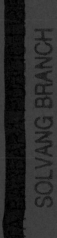

PAUL REVERE

MARTIN LEE

PAUL REVERE

FRANKLIN WATTS
NEW YORK / LONDON / TORONTO / SYDNEY
A FIRST BOOK / 1987

Cover photograph courtesy of The Granger Collection, New York.
Photographs courtesy of The Collections of the Library of Congress:
pp. 14, 18, 21, 28, 34, 38, 44, 47, 69, 80; The Bettmann Archive:
pp. 30, 71; The Metropolitan Museum of Art, bequest of Charles
Allen Munn, 1924: p. 35; Museum of Fine Arts, Boston: pp. 39, 45;
The New York Public Library: pp. 42, 76; Boston Public Library:
pp. 48, 49; New York Public Library Picture Collection: p. 59.

Library of Congress Cataloging-in-Publication Data

Lee, Martin.
Paul Revere.
(A First book)
Bibliography: p.
Includes index.
Summary: A biography of the Revolutionary War
patriot who was also a renowned silversmith.
1. Revere, Paul, 1735-1818—Juvenile literature.
2. Statesmen—Massachusetts—Biography—Juvenile
literature.   3. Massachusetts—Biography—Juvenile
literature.   4. Massachusetts—History—Revolution,
1775-1783—Juvenile literature.   [1. Revere, Paul,
1735-1818.   2. United States—History—Revolution,
1775-1783—Biography.   3. Silversmiths]   I. Title.
F69.R43L44   1987   973.3'311'0924   [B]   86-23362
ISBN 0-531-10312-9

For Charlene Lee Schreiberg

CONTENTS

PAUL REVERE

During his lifetime, Paul Revere
was known as a tireless patriot who
did whatever was asked of him.
He was thought to be a man of
integrity and generosity. His work
as a silversmith was highly regarded.

Today he is remembered most for
what he did one moonlit spring night.
That night, Paul Revere became a
symbol for Americans forever.

This is his story.

APOLLOS RIVOIRE
COMES TO AMERICA

1

Apollos Rivoire was thirteen years old when he arrived in the town of Boston. He was sent there, by way of his uncle's house on the English island of Guernsey, to start a new life in a new world. Apollos's family remained in France, hoping for a better life for their son.

When Apollos left France, he left behind terrible religious persecution. France was primarily a Catholic country, and the French Catholics were mistreating the Protestants who lived there. Apollos's family was Protestant. French Protestants, known as Huguenots, were leaving France by the hundreds of thousands.

The month-long North Atlantic sea voyage was a hard one. It was too cold to spend a lot of time on deck. Apollos spent much of the journey in his damp, dark cabin.

It was the middle of the winter of 1716 when the great ship gracefully sailed into Massachusetts Bay. It passed right by the English fort on Castle Island. Off in the distance

Paul Revere

was the hilly town of Boston, linked to the mainland by a thin strip of land. Apollos saw it all. Boston must have looked very much like other ports he had seen. There was smoke rising from many chimneys. A number of church steeples rose above the buildings.

Apollos got a better look as the ship pulled up alongside Long Wharf, all two thousand feet of it jutting out into the harbor. The other piers were crowded with ships of all kinds. There were whalers, merchant ships, schooners, and ketches. It certainly was a lively place. People hustled about. Porters arrived in their leather aprons as the ship came in to dock. Apollos saw merchants wearing fine lace and stylish wigs step out from their places of business to have a look at the great oceangoing ship. Dogs ran around barking everywhere. And everywhere were the smells of the wharf—of fish drying and bread baking, of rum and tar.

Apollos Rivoire had arrived in America. He was alone and far from home. But he was not the first Huguenot to land in Boston. Many others had come before him, welcomed by the New Englanders who were not at all friendly toward the French. The town of Boston was part of an English colony, and England and France were in constant disagreement about the settlement of North America. The French Catholics who settled in Canada were thought of as enemies.

Apollos's future had been planned for him. His uncle, who had paid for the sea voyage, also had arranged and paid for Apollos to be an apprentice to a silversmith in Boston. This was a typical situation for a boy of thirteen who needed to be trained in a trade.

In this training system, a master artisan took a boy into his household, fed him, clothed him, and taught him his craft. For many years, the boy would be an apprentice, receiving no pay, but learning a great deal. Once the apprenticeship was over, the young man could hire himself out to another artisan, or even start his own shop.

The system had been working this way for many generations in Europe and then spread to America. During Apollos's later years, it began to break down because of the tremendous demand for artisans. Men with little training and inferior skills competed with established craftsmen. America was an open society. Men could enter any business or practice any craft they chose.

Apollos apprenticed for a man named John Coney. Coney, one of about thirty metalsmiths then working in Boston, had an excellent reputation. He was a quiet, religious man who would not tolerate laziness. But he was fair to Apollos and taught him well. It was a good arrangement for both of them.

Apollos learned to speak English and developed enough skill as a silversmith to open his own shop by the time he was twenty-eight years old. He was a quiet, hardworking, determined fellow. He married Deborah Hitchbourn, who came from a large Boston family, and changed his name to Revere so it could be pronounced more easily by Bostonians.

At the end of December, 1734, Deborah gave birth to their second child, a healthy vigorous boy. They named him Paul Revere.

A THRIVING PORT CITY

—2—

Even though eighteenth-century cities were more like large towns by today's standards, the Boston of Paul's childhood was a noisy, active, crowded place. It was particularly crowded with dogs. In fact, there were so many dogs that an ordinance was passed saying that no one could own a dog that was taller than eleven inches!

The narrow, crooked streets—and there were only about a hundred of them—were busy with pedestrians sidestepping the horsecarts and freight wagons. Speeding was definitely a problem; children were always in danger of falling under onrushing hooves or wheels.

Life in a city like Boston was not particularly tied to the rhythms of nature. Women went out shopping from store to store two or three times each week. They could buy meat, vegetables, cheese, and butter at well-stocked stores or at markets. They went to the dry goods store for their cloth, which would be made into clothing for their families.

The birthplace of Paul Revere

They could hire seamstresses for their garments and milliners to make their hats. Men could even buy wood already chopped.

To some extent, though, people's lives were influenced by the seasons. Weather determined sailing schedules, which affected the merchants. Women preserved food for the winter during the late summer and autumn. Still, there were no fields to tend, and everybody had some leisure time. Some people had farms further out. There was time for playing cards, reading, and going to plays and concerts. Dances were popular; so were walks about town or rides in the country.

Another feature of city life was that people had contact with the world beyond their homes. Newspapers provided news from England and from the other colonies, in addition to covering what was happening locally. The papers were often read aloud in taverns. Contact with the outside world had its disadvantages, too. For one thing, it brought sickness. When sailors stepped ashore, they sometimes carried deadly diseases with them, such as smallpox and yellow fever.

The people who lived in Boston faced a housing shortage. There just was not that much space. The two- and three-story wooden and brick houses shared common walls. Mixed in among the houses were shops, taverns, warehouses, stables, and the occasional church and assembly hall.

Laborers and seamen usually lived in rented rooms or in cottages in the back alleys. Some poor people lived on the outskirts of the city. They had vegetable gardens or small farms. Some of Boston's wealthiest people lived on fashionable estates in the surrounding countryside. This upper class, which consisted of import and export merchants, doctors and lawyers, and American and British officials, imitated the life style of the English gentry. They had elegant homes, wore the latest English and French fashions, and spent much of their time visiting one another and entertaining at lavish balls and dinners.

Shopkeepers and artisans, like Paul's father, were not as envious of the rich as they might have been. They lived in modest comfort by today's standards, but were far better off than if they had been living in Europe. Typically, they had small, narrow houses that were about twenty feet wide, perhaps twenty-five feet deep, and one and one-half to two stories high. The shop was generally in the downstairs front room. Sometimes the backyard had a chicken house or a cowshed or even a small garden. Usually, these houses had no carpets or upholstered furniture, and no mirrors or fine glass.

Paul Revere's family lived in a house on Fish Street near the wharves. It was probably similar to the one just described. As a small child, Paul would have spent most of his time in the kitchen, for that was the main living room. As he played on its wooden floor, he would be able to hear the sounds of the wooden and steel hammers from his father's shop. He could also smell the charcoal as the silver was being melted down in the furnace. Closer were the sweet smells of pudding cooking and flannel drying, as well as the fine aroma of lamb or duck roasting.

Paul and the brothers and sisters he now had slept in the attic. At night they could hear the sea lapping against the piers along Clark's Wharf behind the house. They could hear the ships' bells tolling the hours. Paul's father's silversmith shop was well-located down by the wharves, for the

A view of the town of Boston.

silversmith business was dependent upon the shipping trade.

When Paul was growing up, large oceangoing ships came and went frequently, while countless smaller vessels sailed in and out of the harbor. Although the Massachusetts colony could not trade directly with England, it developed a complicated trading system involving the French and Spanish colonies in the West Indies.

Among other things, the New Englanders shipped salt fish, beef, pork, leather goods, horses and some cattle, and staves (wooden ribs) for molasses barrels to the West Indies. In return, they received rice, limes, raisins, and, more important, molasses. Molasses was a key ingredient for making rum, and they liked rum in Massachusetts. Using the profits they made from this trade, the colonists bought goods from the mother country. English ships hauled coffee, tea, ribbons, ironware, paper, glass, and other precious items into the port of Boston. But that is not all that was brought in. A curious boy strolling along the wharves could see some very unusual things in addition to the parades and fireworks that went on. There were dolls all dressed up in European fashions. There were acrobats. There were polar bears and monkeys and dogs that could do amazing things. Once there was even a pickled pirate's head on display!

Sea trade was Boston's livelihood, and Paul's father did well by it. The merchants and sea captains loved fine silver and had the money to pay for it. Paul and his brothers and sisters were raised in what was at that time considered to be comfort and security.

PAUL GROWS UP

—3—

Like many other young boys, Paul was sent to school. He learned manners and some reading skills at an infant school. He and the others sat on wooden benches and memorized the alphabet at a cost to his family of about a penny a week.

When Paul was seven or eight years old, he began attending what was called a writing school. Sons of artisans usually attended these schools. Boys who were being prepared to go to Harvard and then enter the professions went to Latin schools such as North Latin.

Paul went to North Writing, a two-story boy's public school in which writing was taught on one floor and reading on the other. Compared to today's schools, the teaching methods were severe and primitive, and the education the boys received was basic, at best. But at the time, North Writing and its master were very well-respected.

To be accepted into North Writing, a boy had only to show that he could read the psalms. He also had to come up with five shillings to help pay for the heating of the building. The town paid the master's salary.

Boys usually attended these writing schools for perhaps five years, until they were thirteen, or so. That is when their apprenticeships generally began. During those five years, they were in school all year round, breaking only for a few special holidays, and an occasional terrible fire. At that time, fires were devastating for Bostonians and their wooden houses. Fire prevention and fire-fighting techniques were not nearly as effective as they are today.

Like the other boys, Paul was finished with his formal schooling when he was thirteen. Although he had only a meager education by modern standards, he could read and write letters as well as other young men of his time. He could read well enough to understand material related to the work of a silversmith.

Boston was a busy place when Paul was growing up, and he was one of its busiest young citizens. He was curious and energetic, and always looking for something else to do. For instance, Paul and a group of six friends formed a "society" and arranged to ring the bells at Christ Church. There were lots of churches in Boston and each one had a steeple with a bell. Christ Church had eight bells. The boys drew up the contract themselves. Christ Church was not the church Paul's family attended and helped support with four schillings' donation each week. But it had an organ and sweet, clear bells that could be heard all over Boston and across the river to Cambridge and Charlestown.

About the time of Paul's bell-ringing job, a preacher named Jonathan Mayhew was stirring things up with his sermons at the West Street Church. This was in 1750, when Paul Revere was fifteen years old. That year was the one-hundred-year anniversary of the trial and beheading of King Charles I, following the English Civil War. In celebration of that event, Mr. Mayhew spoke out against tyranny and criticized those who did not oppose it. He even supported chopping off the heads of kings, if necessary.

Mayhew's speeches got the people of Boston very excited. Many people approved. Some even said that it was Jonathan Mayhew who fired the first gun of the Revolution. (Actually, Mayhew died before the Revolution began.) It is suspected that young, square-shouldered Paul, eager for excitement and curious about new ideas, was present at these sermons. It would have been a bold step for a boy to take.

It was in his spare time that Paul did his bell-ringing or listened to political speeches. Most of his time was taken up by his apprenticeship. Since leaving school, Paul had been working side by side with his father to learn the silversmith trade. He worked long hours and he worked hard. It was what he wanted to do. He learned to make many things, including teapots, spoons, punch bowls, cups, shoe buckles, bracelets, earrings and lockets, buttons, medals, and spatulas. Right from the start, he showed a great talent for the work. By the time of his father's death in 1754, Paul was already an outstanding craftsman.

A SUMMER SPENT
AT LAKE GEORGE

—4—

After his father's death, Paul took over the responsibilities
of the shop. With his brother Thomas as his apprentice,
and his mother's help, he managed the affairs of the house.
His older sister, Deborah, was about to get married. His
young brother, John, was an apprentice to a tailor. His two
younger sisters helped his mother. Although the family was
not wealthy, the rent got paid when it was due and things
ran rather smoothly. Then, about two years later, Paul
caught a whiff of the excitement in the air and heard the
beating of the drums in the street signaling the call for volunteers to fight the French.

Still at war with England, the French troops and their
Indian allies had come down from Canada to raid the British colonies. Massachusetts was vulnerable to attack. There
were bloody and bitter skirmishes. Lone farmers were
slaughtered in surprise raids as they worked their fields.
The English colonists were furious! When the call to arms

came, Paul was ready. He was the sort of man who always did what had to be done. And he had a score to settle with the French. He remembered stories his father told him about how it was for his family back in France. Although Paul was against war, he traded his apron, anvil, and hammer for the blue and red uniform of a second lieutenant of artillery. It was the spring of 1756. Paul was twenty-one.

Supplied with a gun, a powder horn, a bullet pouch, a knapsack, two spoons, and a wooden bottle for rum, Paul followed the muster captain on the long muddy march westward. The volunteers, with their supply wagons, cannon, oxen, and packhorses, trudged first to the Dutch town of Albany, where they rested their aching feet and met up with troops from other colonies.

From Albany, Paul marched north with the men to Fort William Henry on Lake George. The entire journey covered a distance of two hundred miles. The remainder of the summer and fall were spent at the fort. It was hot, muggy, and boring. Aside from hearing of occasional small Indian raiding parties, Paul and the others saw little action. They spent the summer felling trees, cleaning their rifles, and scratching insect bites. There may not have been enough to do that summer, but there certainly were enough black flies.

Although Paul was the sort of man who seemed to adapt to whatever was happening, he was having a particularly miserable time at Lake George. He much preferred the sounds of the city to the war whoops of the unseen Indians and the howling of the wolves. When the time came to leave the fort behind, Paul was ready.

It was not until November that the line of ragged, angry soldiers in their summer uniforms made the long cold

*The defeat of General Braddock in
the French and Indian War*

march back to Boston. All along the way, Paul thought of the sounds and smells of the life he missed. He longed to hear the crying of seagulls by the shore, and the rattle of wagons, and the clatter of hooves on the cobblestone streets. He missed the creaking of the wooden machinery and the tapping of hammers. He missed the sounds of drummers drumming up business. He thought of the smells of ale brewing and leather being made. He thought of the smells near his house by Clark's Wharf—the scents of coffee, spices, and fish. He also missed hearing the bells—the great bells of Christ Church and King's Chapel, and the smaller school bells and cowbells. He could not wait to get back.

Paul was twenty-two when he returned from the war. He was a changed man. He had taken and given too many orders. He was more than ready to get back to work.

Paul returned to find that his mother and Thomas had kept the shop going during his absence. But he had been missed. A good look at the account ledgers told him that. So he plunged back into the work. It certainly felt good to grip a hammer firmly again.

His work was now better than ever. By 1757, Paul was a master silversmith, quickly becoming one of the very best in the colonies. And business was good, not only for Paul's shop, but all over. Manufacturing, shipping, and farming had grown. Overseas trade flourished. More people had money to spend on silver. Lots of orders came Paul's way for his highly regarded work. It was all he could do to keep up.

Not long after his return, Paul married Sara Orne, a young, frail woman he knew from his church. Soon after that, the house began to get crowded with children. Sara

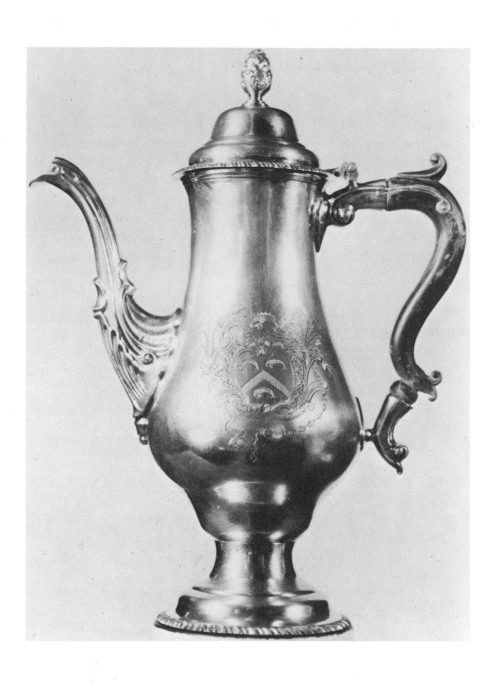

gave birth to a child almost every other year. Deborah was the first. Then came Paul, Sara, Mary, Frances, and Elizabeth. There were nine mouths to feed, including Paul's mother, who lived in the house with them. Paul worked tirelessly to support them. Except for a smallpox epidemic that hit Boston in 1763, things went along fairly comfortably for all the Reveres.

A silver teapot by Revere.
He was a master silversmith.

HATED TAXES AND
SECRET MEETINGS

5

The war with the French finally ended. With it went the prosperity of the war years. Economic depression set in heavily upon the colonists. The English Parliament was blamed for the suffering.

But the English were busy with their own troubles. Parliament had to raise money to pay the costs of the war and to pay for keeping an army of ten thousand troops in America for protection against the Indians. The English people were already being heavily taxed. The English government wanted the colonists to pay a share of the cost. With this in mind, Parliament was determined to enforce some old shipping laws. But more money was still needed. Parliament made some new laws. It passed the Stamp Act, the first direct tax on the American people.

The Stamp Act declared that all printed matter, everything from a newspaper to a marriage license, could not be sold without a stamp. Some colonists were furious and cried out in protest. They did not like having to obey laws their own representatives had no say in passing. The saying "taxation without representation is tyranny" became a rallying cry. People began to organize to talk about what they could do to change these new laws. Parliament's actions went against the new ways of governing that were beginning to take root in the colonies.

Political clubs, falling generally within two opposing groups, began to form. On one side were the Tories, and on the other side, the Whigs. The Tories were loyal to the king of England. They believed that the colonies would be better off if they remained part of the English empire. The Tories thought England had every right to tax them. The Whigs, or Patriots, on the other hand, believed that the colonies could get along just fine without the presence of English soldiers and warships. They did not want any meddling with colonial affairs. But most of all, they did not want to be taxed.

Paul Revere listened to all the talk. He listened to men like James Otis, who spoke out against the harsh methods England was using to enforce the tax laws. He listened to more radical men such as Sam Adams and Dr. Joseph Warren, who went even further and favored independence. Paul listened to many Whig leaders and liked what he heard. He joined a few Whig clubs, and nearly every evening he could be found meeting secretly in the back rooms of taverns. He was already a member of the well-established, orderly society of Masons. He now joined the extremely secret Long Room Club, of which he was the only artisan member. He listened eagerly and attentively to brilliant colonial leaders planning for the future. Like them, Paul felt his political rights had been threatened.

Soon Paul began to make friends with the political

affix the STAMP.

This is the Place to

The tax imposed by the British
caused dissension in the colonies.
Opposite: Sam Adams

leaders. This dark, stocky, young silversmith was beginning to stand out. Though he himself made no famous speeches, he was beginning to gain recognition as a capable, cool-headed man who could get things done. Paul Revere was a man worth watching.

One thing these secret clubs did was to stage political protests. Once they hung a large boot from a giant elm. The boot had a devil inside peering out. A stuffed dummy was hung next to the boot. These effigies represented two men—Lord Bute, the king's minister, who pushed strongly for the Stamp Act, and Andrew Oliver, the local official whose job it was to distribute the stamps. The people of Boston were caught by surprise. But not Paul—he already knew about it. He knew because he became a member of the Sons of Liberty.

Directed by the Long Room Club, the Sons of Liberty was a secret society devoted to finding clever ways to pester the English and harass colonial officials who enforced English laws. Paul Revere was now into politics up to his square shoulders.

Paul's political activity took place mostly in the evenings. His days were spent finding new ways to feed all those mouths at home. This was no easy task. Silversmiths suffered along with everyone else, as silver was a luxury during those hard times. Money was scarce. In fact, some of his customers paid him in rum or in fish.

But, as always, Paul did what he had to do. He taught himself to engrave copper plates. He even became a political cartoonist. Though he did not have much talent for drawing, his work reflected what many people were thinking, and he achieved a certain amount of success. One cartoon showed those effigies hanging from the giant elm.

That tree became known as the Liberty Tree. Soon, most colonies had one of their own.

For a busy man, this was a particularly busy time. Before Paul finished one thing, he was on to something else. One of his ledgers began: "This is my book for me to. . . ." Before he had finished that sentence, he was involved with another task. It seems as if there was always more to do than there were hours in the day. Even so, Paul added another skill to his list of talents—dentistry. This was not dentistry as we know it today. In colonial times, when people had toothaches, the teeth were pulled. There were no fillings. Paul learned from John Baker, an English surgeon dentist, how to make false teeth and fasten them in with silver wires. He learned to carve these teeth from ivory. He used sheep's teeth, too. He even used hippopotamus tusks. Here is one of his advertisements, which ran in the *Boston Gazette*:

> WHEREAS many Persons are so unfortunate as to lose their Fore-Teeth by Accident and otherways, to their great Detriment, not only in Looks, but in speaking both in Public and Private:—This is to inform all such, that they may have them replaced with artificial ones, that looks as well as Natural, & answer the End of Speaking to all Intents, by PAUL REVERE Goldsmith, near the Head of Dr. Clark's Wharf, Boston.

Paul was successful at dentistry. But after a few years he stopped practicing, because his real interest and skill were in silver work, not in making copper plates or installing false teeth.

Above: the colonists rebelled.
Opposite: Revere as painted by the famous
artist, John Singleton Copley

One of Paul's customers was the well-known portrait painter John Singleton Copley. Copley's paintings have shown us what many of the leading colonists looked like. He painted Paul's friend Joseph Warren's portrait, and Sam Adams's, as well. Paul often made the frames for Copley's miniatures. One day the men agreed that Copley would paint Revere's portrait.

This artist's subjects usually posed in their finest clothes. But Paul was painted as he was, at work on a tea-pot. He did not powder his hair, as was the custom, nor did he wear his coat. He sat on his workbench in his shirt-sleeves with his collar open. His tools lay on the worktable before him. Copley, who was famous for his ability to paint people as they really were, captured on canvas Paul's self-confidence and seriousness.

BLOODSHED ON KING STREET

—6—

In 1768, the same year Paul ran his dentistry ad, a fleet of British warships entered Boston's harbor. The troops they delivered were sent not so much to protect the colonists from Indian raids, but rather to police the town. They arrived to settle down the noisy street marches and other annoying activities of the Sons of Liberty, and to see that tax money was collected.

Just the sight of the British "regulars" and their red uniforms was enough to disgust a number of the colonists. Those, like Paul Revere, who remembered the French and Indian War miseries, were particularly unhappy. So were the soldiers, many of whom did not want to be in Boston in the first place. They were about as comfortable with the citizens of Boston as Paul Revere was with the ticks and flies of Lake George. The soldiers wanted to be in Europe, where the more highly regarded officers and troops were sent to fight.

British soldiers encamped on Boston Commons

The Sons of Liberty decided to pursue a course of non-violence. But they also decided not to cooperate with the soldiers, and to make life as difficult for them as they could. Everyone but the rich colonists resented the presence of the troops.

Some of the soldiers who resented their assignments in Boston deserted. Those who did not desert could not manage to keep on good terms with the townspeople. For one thing, the recently passed Quartering Act forced the colonists to provide housing for the soldiers. For another thing, soldiers, who had very little to do, took on odd jobs for meals or very low pay. This angered colonial workmen for whom times were hard and jobs scarce.

For the most part, things went along peacefully for a while. To be sure, there were angry words and insults hurled back and forth. There were tavern brawls and some street fighting. The soldiers were constantly taunted by the young boys of the town who called them "bloody-backs" and "lobsters for sale." There was a great deal of bad feeling, but no shots were fired. Some folks even benefited by having the troops around. Trade picked up a little, and for some, the social life was more lively. Paul Revere, who on some evenings marched in protest with the Sons of Liberty, actually made some money by selling a series of engravings he made to the troops landing.

But things were not really as normal as they seemed. Boston was like a powder keg waiting to explode. Hostility simmered for about eighteen months. Then the explosion came.

The date was Monday, March 5, 1770. It had been snowing, and about a foot had accumulated on the ground. Early in the day there was a fight between some soldiers

John Lamb speaking at a
Sons of Liberty meeting at
New York's City Hall

Another example of Revere's work as a silversmith—the Liberty bowl, made for members of the Sons of Liberty

and local workmen. Tempers were flaring. Later in the day, a boy who had been insulting a sentry on King Street was knocked to the ground. The boy ran off to gather some support, then returned to continue the abuse. More people arrived, and that lone sentry, who had been pelted with ice and snow and oyster shells many times before, was getting it worse than he was accustomed to. He began to lose his temper.

The sentry, now faced with an angry mob, threatened to shoot anyone who came too close. Crispus Attucks, a huge ex-slave, did just that, taunting the nervous soldier as he approached him. The sentry was terrified. But instead of firing, he called for help. His cry brought Captain Preston and seven regulars. Everybody was tense as the nine soldiers gathered in a group and loaded their muskets.

Then the crowd began to jostle again and rush in upon the soldiers. They were face to face with them, swinging sticks and fists. Some townspeople tried to reason with the mob, to get them to pull back. But it was too late. The words "Present . . ." and "Fire" were heard. Then a volley of shots rang out. When it was over—and it was over quickly—four men lay dead in the snow, another lay dying, and a number of others were wounded.

Captain Preston worked frantically to stop the shooting, finally succeeding. The crowd hustled about in confusion, tripping over one another in their haste to get away. Other people poured out into the streets to find out what was going on. Not many seemed to know what had actually happened. Finally the crowd dispersed and people returned to their houses. Preston and his eight men were arrested and placed in jail before the night was over. They would be held and tried for their actions.

The massacre in Boston in 1770

BOSTON, March 12.

THE Town of Boston affords a recent and
melancholy Demonstration of the destructive
Consequences of quartering Troops among
Citizens in a Time of Peace, under a Pretence
of supporting the Laws and aiding Civil Authority; every considerate and unprejudic'd
among us was deeply imprest with the Apprehen-
these Consequences when it was known that a
er of Regiments were ordered to this Town under
Pretext, but in Reality to inforce oppressive Mea-
to awe & controul the legislative as well as exe-
Power of the Province, and to quell a Spirit of
y, which however it may have been basely oppos'd
en ridicul'd by some, would do Honor to any Age
ntry. A few Persons amongst us had determin'd
all their Influence to procure so destructive a Mea-
ith a View to their securely enjoying the Profits of
merican Revenue, and unhappily both for Britain
is Country they found Means to effect it.
s to Governor Bernard, the Commissioners, their
dents and Coadjutors, that we are indebted as the
ing Cause of a military Power in this Capital—
Boston Journal of Occurrences, as printed in Mr.
York Gazette, from Time to Time, afforded many
g Instances of the Distresses brought upon the In-
nts by this Measure; and since those Journals have
discontinued, our Troubles from that Quarter have
growing upon us: We have known a Party of Sol
n the face of Day fire off a loaden Musket upon the
itants, others have been prick'd with Bayonets,
ven our Magistrates assaulted and put in Danger of
Lives, when Offenders brought before them have
rescued; and why those and other bold and base
nals have as yet escaped the Punishment due to their
s, may be soon Matter of Enquiry by the Represen-
Body of this People——It is natural to suppose that
the Inhabitants of this Town saw those Laws which
been enacted for their Security, and which they
ambitious of holding up to the Soldiery, eluded,
should more commonly resent for themselves—
ccordingly it has so happened; many have been the
bles between them and the Soldiery; but it seems
being often worsted by our Youth in those Rencoun-
has only serv'd to irritate the former—What passed at
Gray's Rope-walk, has already been given the Pub-
may be said to have led the Way to the late Catastro-
That the Rope-walk Lads when attacked by supe-
Numbers should defend themselves with so much Spi-
d Success in the Club-way, was too mortifying, and
ps it may hereafter appear, that even some of their
rs were unhappily affected with this Circumstance:
Stories were propagated among the Soldiery, that
to agitate their Spirits; particularly on the Sab-
that one Chambers, a Sergeant, represented as a
Man, had been missing the preceeding Day, and
therefore have been murdered by the Townsmen;
fficer of Distinction so far credited this Report,
e enter'd Mr. Gray's Rope-walk that Sabbath; and
required of by that Gentleman as soon as he could
him, the Occasion of his so doing, the Officer re-
, that it was to look if the Serjeant said to be mur-
had not been hid there; this sober Serjeant was
d on the Monday unhurt, in a House of Pleasure—
Evidences already collected shew, that many Threat-
had been thrown out by the Soldiery, but we do
retend to say that there was any preconcerted Plan,
the Evidences are published, the World will judge—
may however venture to declare, that it appears too
ble from their Conduct, that some of the Soldiery
d to draw and provoke the Townsmen into Squabbles,
hat they then intended to make Use of other Wea-
than Canes, Clubs or Bludgeons.
r Readers will doubtless expect a circumstantial Ac-
t of the tragical Affair on Monday Night last; but
pe they will excuse our being so particular as we
d have been, had we not seen that the Town
ntending an Enquiry & full Representation thereof.
the Evening of Monday, being the 5th Current,
al Soldiers of the 29th Regiment were seen parading
treets with their drawn Cutlasses and Bayonets,
g and wounding Numbers of the Inhabitants.
few minutes after nine o'clock, four youths,
d Edward Archbald, William Merchant,
cis Archbald, and John Leech, jun. came
Cornhill together, and seperating at Doctor
g's corner, the two former were passing
arrow alley leading to Murray's barrack, in
h was a soldier brandishing a broad sword of
common size against the walls, out of which
ruck fire plentifully. A person of a mean counte-
e armed with a large cudgel bore him company.
ard Archbald admonished Mr. Merchant to take
of the sword, on which the soldier turned round
struck Archbald on the arm, then pushed at
chant and pierced thro' his cloaths inside the
close to the arm-pit and grazed the skin. Mer-
t then struck the soldier with a short stick he
& the other Person ran to the barrack & bro't
him two soldiers, one armed with a pair of
s the other with a shovel: he with the tongs
ed Archbald back thro' the alley, collar'd and
im over the head with the tongs. The noise
people together, and John Hicks, a young lad,
g up, knock'd the soldier down, but let him
p again; and more lads gathering, drove them
to the barrack, where the boys stood some time
were to keep them in. In less than a minute
12 of them came out with drawn cutlasses,
and bayonets, and set upon the unarmed boys
young folks, who stood them a little while, but
g the inequality of their equipment dispersed.
hearing the noise, one Samuel Atwood,
up to see what was the matter, and enter-
he alley from dock-square, heard the lat-

ter part of the combat, and when the boys had dispersed he met the 10 or 12 soldiers aforesaid rushing down the alley towards the square, and asked them if they intended to murder people? They answered Yes, by G—d, root and branch! With that one of them struck Mr. Atwood with a club, which was repeated by another, and being unarmed he turned to go off, and received a wound on the left shoulder which reached the bone and gave him much pain. Retreating a few steps, Mr. Atwood met two officers and said, Gentlemen, what is the matter? They answered, you'll see by and by. Immediately after, those heroes appeared in the square, asking where were the boogers? where were the cowards? But notwithstanding their fierceness to naked men, one of them advanced towards a youth who had a split of a raw stave in his hand, and said damn them here is one of them; but the young man seeing a person near him with a drawn sword and good cane ready to support him, held up his stave in defiance, and they quietly passed by him up the little alley by Mr. Silsby's to Kingstreet, where they attacked single and unarmed persons till they raised much clamor, and then turned down Cornhill street, insulting all they met in like manner, and pursuing some to their very doors. Thirty or forty persons, mostly lads, being by this means gathered in Kingstreet, Capt. Preston, with a party of men with charged bayonets, came from the main guard to the Commissioners house, the soldiers pushing their bayonets, crying, Make way! They took place by the custom-house, and continuing to push to drive the people off, pricked some in several places; on which they were clamorous, and, it is said, threw snow-balls. On this, the Captain commanded them to fire, and more snow-balls coming, he again said, Damn you, Fire, be the consequence what it will! One soldier then fired, and a townsman with a cudgel struck him over the hands with such force that he dropt his firelock; and rushing forward aimed a blow at the Captain's head, which graz'd his hat and fell pretty heavy upon his arm: However, the soldiers continued the fire, successively, till 7 or 8, or as some say 11 guns were discharged.

By this fatal manœuvre, three men were laid dead on the spot, and two more struggling for life; but what shewed a degree of cruelty unknown to British troops, at least since the house of Hanover has directed their operations, was an attempt to fire upon or push with their bayonets the persons who undertook to remove the slain and wounded!

Mr. Benjamin Leigh, now undertaker in the Delph Manufactory, came up, and after some conversation with Capt. Preston, relative to his conduct in this affair, advised him to draw off his men, with which he complied.

The dead are Mr. Samuel Gray, killed on the spot, the ball entering his head and beating off a large portion of his skull.

A mulatto man, named Crispus Attucks, who was born in Framingham, but lately belonged to New-Providence and was here in order to go for North-Carolina, also killed instantly; two balls entering his breast, one of them in special goring the right lobe of the lungs, and a great part of the liver most horribly.

Mr. James Caldwell, mate of Capt. Morton's vessel, in like manner killed by two balls entering his back.

Mr. Samuel Maverick, a promising youth of 17 years of age, son of the widow Maverick, and an apprentice to Mr. Greenwood, Ivory-Turner, mortally wounded, a ball went through his belly, & was cut out at his back: He died the next morning.

A lad named Christopher Monk, about 17 years of age, an apprentice to Mr. Walker, Shipwright; wounded, a ball entered his back about 4 inches above the left kidney, near the spine, and was cut out of the breast on the same side; apprehended he will die.

A lad named John Clark, about 17 years of age, whose parents live at Medford, and an apprentice to Capt. Samuel Howard of this town; wounded, a ball entered just above his groin and came out at his hip, on the opposite side, apprehended he will die.

Mr. Edward Payne, of this town, Merchant, standing at his entry-door, received a ball in his arm, which shattered some of the bones.

Mr. John Green, Taylor, coming up Leverett's Lane, received a ball just under his hip, and lodged in the under part of his thigh, which was extracted.

Mr. Robert Patterson, a seafaring man, who was the person that had his trowsers shot through in Richardson's affair, wounded; a ball went through his right arm, and he suffered great loss of blood.

Mr. Patrick Carr, about 30 years of age, who work'd with Mr. Field, Leather Breeches-maker in Queen street, wounded, a ball enter'd near his hip and went out at his side.

A lad named David Parker, an apprentice to Mr. Eddy the Wheelwright, wounded, a ball entered in his thigh.

The People were immediately alarmed with the Report of this horrid Massacre, the Bells were set a Ringing, and great Numbers soon assembled at the Place where this tragical Scene had been acted; their Feelings may be better conceived than express'd; and while some were taking Care of the Dead and Wounded, the Rest were in Consultation what to do in those dreadful Circumstances.—But so little intimidated were they, notwithstanding their being within a few Yards of the Main-Guard, and seeing the 29th Regiment under Arms, and drawn up in King-Street; that they kept their Station and appear'd as an Officer of Rank express'd it, ready to run upon the very Muzzles of their Muskets.—The Lieut. Governor soon came into the Town-House, and there met some of his Majesty's Council, and a Number of Civil Magistrates; a considerable Body of the People immediately entered the Council Chamber, and expressed themselves to his Honor with a Freedom and Warmth becoming the occasion. He used his utmost Endeavours to pacify them, requesting that they would let the Matter subside for the Night, and promising to do all in his Power that Justice should be done, and the Law have its Course; Men of Influence and Weight with the People were not wanting on their part to procure their Compliance with his Honor's Request, by representing the horrible Consequences of a promiscuous and rash Engagement in the Night, and assuring them that such Measures should be entered upon in the Morning, as would be agreeable to their Dignity, and a more likely way of obtaining the best Satisfaction for the Blood of their Fellow-Townsmen.—The Inhabitants attended to these Suggestions, and the Regiment under Arms being ordered to their Barracks, which was insisted upon by the People, they then separated & returned to their Dwellings by One o'Clock. At 3 o'Clock Capt. Preston was committed, as were the Soldiers who fir'd, a few Hours after him.

Tuesday Morning presented a most shocking Scene, the Blood of our Fellow Citizens running like Water thro' King-Street, and the Merchants Exchange the principal Spot of the Military Parade for about 18 Months past. Our Blood might also be track'd up to the Head of Long-Lane, and through divers other Streets and Passages.

At eleven o'clock the inhabitants met at Faneuil-Hall, and after some animated speeches becoming the occasion, they chose a Committee of 15 respectable Gentlemen to wait upon the Lieut. Governor in Council, to request of him to issue his Orders for the immediate removal of the troops.

The Message was in these Words:

THAT it is the unanimous opinion of this meeting that the inhabitants and soldiery can no longer live together in safety; that nothing can rationally be expected to restore the peace of the town & prevent further blood & carnage, but the immediate removal of the Troops; and that we therefore most fervently pray his Honor that his power and influence may be exerted for their instant removal.

His Honor's Reply, which was laid before the Town then Adjourn'd to the Old South Meeting-House, was as follows,

Gentlemen,

I AM extremely sorry for the unhappy differences between the inhabitants and troops, and especially for the action of the last evening, and I have exerted myself upon that occasion that a due enquiry may be made, and that the law may have its course. I have in council consulted with the commanding officers of the two regiments who are in the town. They have their orders from the General at New-York. It is not in my power to countermand those orders. The Council have desired that the two regiments may be removed to the Castle. From the particular concern which the 29th regiment has had in your differences, Col. Dalrymple who is the commanding officer of the troops has signified that that regiment shall without delay be placed in the barracks at the Castle until he can send to the General and receive his further orders concerning both the regiments, and that the main guard shall be removed, and the 14th regiment so disposed and laid under such restraint that all occasion of future disturbances may be prevented.

The foregoing Reply having been read and fully considered—the question was put, Whether the Report be satisfactory? Passed in the Negative, (only 1 dissentient.) out of upwards of 4000 Voters.

It was then moved and voted John Hancock, Esq; Mr. Samuel Adams, Mr. William Molineux, William Phillips, Esq; Dr. Joseph Warren, Joshua Henshaw, Esq; and Samuel Pemberton, Esq; be a Committee to wait on his Honour the Lieut. Governor, and inform him, that it is the unanimous Opinion of this Meeting, that the Reply made to a Vote of the Inhabitants presented his Honor in the Morning, is by no Means satisfactory; and that nothing less will satisfy, than a total and immediate removal of all the Troops.

The Committee having waited upon the Lieut. Governor agreeable to the foregoing Vote; laid before the Inhabitants the following Vote of Council received from his Honor.

His Honor the Lieut. Governor laid before the Board a Vote of the Town of Boston, passed this Afternoon, and then addressed the Board as follows,

Gentlemen of the Council,

"I lay before you a Vote of the Town of Boston, which I have just now received from them, and I now ask your Advice what you judge necessary to be done upon it."

The Council thereupon expressed themselves to be *unanimously* of opinion, "that it was absolutely necessary for his Majesty's service, the good order of the Town, and the Peace of the Province, that the Troops should be immediately removed out of the Town of Boston, and thereupon advised his Honor to communicate this Advice of the Council to Col. Dalrymple, and to pray that he would order the Troops down to Castle-William." The Committee also informed the Town, that Col. Dalrymple, after having seen the Vote of Council, said to the Committee, "That he now gave his word of Honor that he would begin his Preparations in the Morning, and that there should be no unnecessary delay until the whole of the two Regiments were removed to the Castle."

Upon the above Report being read, the Inhabitants could not avoid expressing the high Satisfaction it afforded them.

After Measures were taken for the Security of the Town in the Night by a strong Military Watch, the Meeting was Dissolved.

The 29th Regiment have already left us, a
Regiment are following them, so that w
Town will soon be clear of all the Troops.
dom and true Policy of his Majesty's Coun
Dalrymple the Commander appear in this Me
Regiments in the midst of this populous Ci
Inhabitants justly incensed: Those of the n
Towns actually under Arms upon the first I
Massacre, and the Signal only wanting to b
Hours to the Gates of this City many Thou
brave Brethren in the Country, deeply affe
Distresses, and to whom we are greatly obli
Occasion—No one knows where this would
and what important Consequences even t
British Empire might have followed, which
tion & Loyalty upon so trying an Occasion, s
in the Commander's Assurances have happily

Last Thursday, agreeable to a general R
Inhabitants, and by the Consent of Parents
were carried to their *Grave* in Succession,
of *Samuel Gray*, *Samuel Maverick*, *Jam*
and *Crispus Attucks*, the unhappy Victims
the bloody Massacre of the Monday Evening

On this Occasion most of the Shops in
shut, all the Bells were ordered to toll a sol
were also those in the neighboring Towns of
Roxbury, &c. The Procession began to mo
the Hours of 4 and 5 in the Afternoon; tw
fortunate Sufferers, viz. Mess. *James Caldwell*
Attucks, who were Strangers, borne from F
attended by a numerous Train of Persons of
and the other two, viz. Mr. *Samuel Gra*
House of Mr. Benjamin Gray, (his Broth
North-side the Exchange, and Mr. *Maveric*
House of his distressed Mother Mrs. *Mary M*
Union-Street, each followed by their respecti
and Friends: The several Hearses forming
in King-Street, the Theatre of that inhuma
proceeded from thence thro' the Main-Street
by an immense Concourse of People, so nu
be obliged to follow in Ranks of six, and bro
a long Train of Carriages belonging to t
Gentry of the Town. The Bodies were dep
Vault in the middle Burying-ground: The
Circumstances of their Death, the Distress
visible in every Countenance, together with
Solemnity with which the whole Funeral wa
surpass Description.

A military watch has been kept every n
town-house and prison, in which many of th
pectable gentlemen of the town have appe
common soldier, and night after night have
attendance.

A Servant Boy of one Manwaring the Tide-
Quebec is now in Goal, having deposed that h
Order and Encouragement of his Superiors ha
a Musket several Times from one of the Wind
House in King-Street, hired by the Commissione
House Officers to do their Business in; more th
Person swore upon Oath, that they apprehen
Discharges came from that Quarter.—It is w
that we may soon be able to account for the A
Mr. Otis some Time past; the Message by Wilm
from the same House to the infamous Richardso
firing the Gun which kill'd young Snider, and
such a Scene of Villainy acted by a dirty Band
astonish the Public.

It is supposed that there must have been a g
ber of People from Town and Country at th
those who were massacred by the Soldiers, tha
together on this Continent on any Occasion.

A more dreadful Tragedy has been acted by
in King-Street, Boston, New-England, than
since exhibited in St. George's Field, London, in
which may serve instead of Beacons for both

Had those worthy Patriots, not only repre
nard and the Commissioners as a Faction, but
making a Separation between Britain and the
any Thing else in Contemplation than the Pr
our Rights, and bringing Things back to their
tion—What an Opening has been given them

Among other Matters in the Warrant for
Town-Meeting this Day, is the following
"Whether the Town will take any Mea
public Monument may be erected on the Sp
late tragical Scene was acted, as a Memento
of that horrid Massacre, and the destru
quences of Military Troops being quarter
regulated City."

The Transactions of the Town Meetings
Dedham, Bridgwater, &c. compos'd for thi
we are oblig'd to postpone for want of Ro

BOSTON-GOAL, Monday, 12th
Messieurs EDES & GILL.

PERMIT me thro' the Channel of your Pa
my Thanks in the most publick Manner
tants in general of this Town—who thro
Party and Prejudice, have with the utmost
Freedom stept forth Advocates for Truth, in
injured Innocence, in the late unhappy Affair
on Monday Night last: And to assure them
ever have the highest Sense of the Justice t
me, which will be ever gratefully rememb
Their much obliged and most obedient hu
THOMAS P

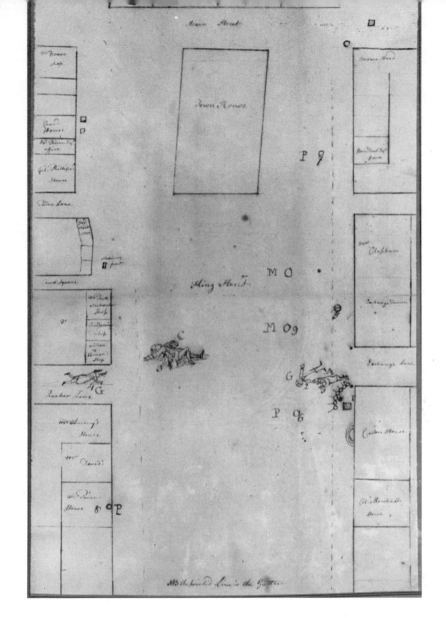

Opposite: a newspaper account of the massacre.
Above: Revere's plan of the scene of the
Boston Massacre, used at the trial of
Captain Preston and the soldiers

It is not known for certain where Paul Revere was that night. He may very well have been on the scene because an accurate pen-and-ink drawing he made was used at the soldiers' trial. This drawing showed exactly where the soldiers stood and where the victims fell.

The massacre was, of course, a big news story. A newspaper, *Boston Gazette*, which came out soon afterward, included an engraving Paul made of the event. This time accuracy was not Paul's main concern. The engraving, one of the most famous of all American engravings, shows an orderly line of British soldiers firing upon a group of non-threatening townspeople standing helplessly a few feet away. Captain Preston is seen with his sabre raised, ordering his men to fire. Crispus Attucks is not portrayed as being black.

Paul's engraving became a valuable piece of Whig propaganda. It added fuel to the fire of anti-British feeling with every copy sold. And, indeed, many copies were sold.

Considering the circumstances, the soldiers involved in the incident got a surprisingly fair trail. The future president, John Adams, and Josiah Quincy defended them. Patrick Carr, who died soon after from a bullet wound, gave honest testimony. The sentry, whose name was Montgomery, and another soldier, named Kilroy, were found guilty. The other seven were found innocent.

The remainder of the soldiers stationed in Boston left town immediately. They went to the fort at nearby Castle Island where they set up temporary quarters.

Coincidentally, on the very same day as the shooting, the English Parliament voted to withdraw all the taxes, *except* one. A tax on tea was left as a token. It was a solitary reminder that England owned the colonies and could levy taxes as Parliament saw fit.

A SPECIAL PARTY

— 7 —

Things quieted down somewhat for Paul Revere during the three years following the bloody encounter on King Street. He went on with his work, drinking *untaxed* Dutch tea and raising his family.

He bought a house on North Square, which was not a square at all. It was, in fact, a triangle. North Square was located a block in from the wharves and was considered a respectable place to live. It also must have been considered a good place to have a market, for one of Boston's colorful, open-air markets was always held there in season.

The openings and closings of the markets were signaled by the ringing of bells. The markets brought together country folk, fishermen, and townspeople for a day of shopping and haggling. Farmers arrived with horses, carts, and baskets loaded down with goods such as grains, butter, and vegetables. There was plenty of wild fowl to buy. There was pork, bear meat, and venison. Naturally, there was an abundance of seafood and fish. Paul occasionally acted as the clerk of these markets, seeing to it that the bargaining went on smoothly and fairly.

It is hard to say where Paul got the time to do it, for, as usual, he was a very busy man. He worked tirelessly in his shop, taking only the customary breaks that artisans took for meals and chats with friends at the tavern. His skills as a silversmith continued to sharpen, and his work got better and better. There was not much he could not or would not do. He made clock faces and he made sword handles. He made everything from babies' rattles to pet collars.

When he was not working, Paul was with his family. When he was not with his family, he was at some secret political meeting. He kept up his membership with the Masons and other clubs. The Sons of Liberty were still in action, and Paul was still a member. In fact, he was now one of the principal members. He was involved in the demonstrations designed to badger and ridicule the merchants who carried on business with England. He took part in the harassing of customs officials. As usual, there were not enough hours in the day for Paul Revere.

In the spring of 1773, soon after giving birth to another daughter, Isanna, Sara Revere died. Isanna lived only until the fall. About a month after the child's death, Paul remarried. The children's new mother was Rachel Walker, a kind and strong young woman who helped during these sad times. It was a good match that worked out well for both people. Paul and Rachel would eventually have eight children together, three of whom died in infancy.

Another thing happened to the Reveres in 1773—Paul bought a horse. In those days, the best way to get news from one place to another was on horseback. Paul soon became known as an outstanding rider.

Meanwhile, in London, the East India Company had a great deal of tea stored up. This powerful company was losing money rapidly, so Parliament decided to ship all the tea to the colonists. When the Sons of Liberty got wind of this, they spread posters around Boston announcing a mass meeting to decide what to do about it. What they decided at the meeting was that the tea must never be unloaded.

The first ship to arrive carrying the unwanted tea, the *Dartmouth*, docked at Griffin's Wharf that November, 1773. Paul Revere was among the twenty-five armed men posted there to see that the cargo remained locked in chests on board. Paul stayed up all night guarding the ship. The following morning, at another meeting, the patriots discussed the possibility that the other ships might attempt to unload their tea in other ports. Paul and five others were selected to ride to those port towns to give warning. Paul went home and buckled on his spurs, while young Paul saddled up the horse.

Once again, Paul Revere showed that he would do what had to be done. That morning he took his first ride for the Patriot cause. He would take many more.

Soon the *Dartmouth* was joined by two more ships carrying tea, the *Eleanor* and the *Beaver*. Together, the three vessels were loaded with $90,000 worth of the disputed tea. Groups of citizens kept guard around the clock to make sure none of the tea was unloaded.

The law said that a ship would have its cargo seized and sold at auction if that cargo was not unloaded within twenty days. The colonists did not want this to happen. They insisted that the ships leave the port and return to England. But legally, no ship could leave unless it had unloaded all its freight. The governor of Massachusetts, however, did have the authority to allow ships to leave the port with their cargo still on board.

The British-appointed governor during that time was asked to do this. He denied the request. In fact, Governor Hutchinson instructed the English artillery on Castle Island to fire upon the ships if they left with their tea chests still aboard, unless they had a passport signed by him.

The people of Boston were getting nervous. They wondered what was going to happen when the *Dartmouth*'s stay in port reached its twentieth day. It was a time of nail-biting and a time of doubt. The people wondered what they were getting themselves into.

December 16 was day number nineteen. A mass meeting, attended by thousands of worried townspeople, was held at Old South Church. The colonists nervously listened to a variety of speakers as they awaited the appearance of the ship's captain, who had gone to plead with the governor to allow the *Dartmouth* to sail.

The captain returned with the news that Governor Hutchinson had refused to change his mind. But his refusal did not catch the leaders of the Sons of Liberty by surprise. They expected it and had already hatched a plan. During secret meetings at a tavern called the Green Dragon, they concocted a scheme for getting rid of the tea.

It was early evening when the captain grimly presented the latest news to the leaders. At that point, Sam Adams announced to the crowd that continuing the meeting would not help them to save their country. His words were a signal. Immediately, the building rocked with excitement. People raced into the street shouting, "To Griffin's Wharf!" and "Boston Harbour a tea-pot tonight!" People knew where to go and what to do. First, they hustled off to their houses or to the back rooms of taverns to change their clothing.

They dressed in costumes they usually saved for the exciting Guy Fawkes Day celebrations and the torchlight protest marches led by the Sons of Liberty. They spread grease and soot on their faces as they usually did on those occasions, but this time they smeared on streaks of red paint, too. They pulled stocking caps down low on their heads and some stuck feathers in their hair. Some pulled blankets over their shoulders. Then each of these "Mohawks" headed down to Griffin's Wharf, on what was to become a very important night.

Although they did not look much like Indians, these ordinary townspeople did not look much like themselves, either. They approached the wharves in silence. As part of the disguise, there was no speaking, only grunting. They formed three groups, each having a leader, and boarded the three tea-carrying vessels. Paul Revere was there grunting with the others. Some said that Sam Adams and even the wealthy and influential Patriot John Hancock may have been there, too.

The plan was to dump all the tea into the water. The protestors did not intend to keep any of the tea or damage anything on the boats.

Fearing attack from the British warships anchored nearby, the colonists worked at top speed. As thousands of townspeople gathered on the dock and silently watched, the "Mohawks" went about their business. They hoisted the three-hundred and forty-two tea chests up onto the decks and broke them open with axes. Then they began dumping the entire cargo into the water.

The task took all night to complete. No one was injured. Only one man tried to steal some of the tea. At dawn, the group disbanded. Everyone went home to wipe off the grease and paint, pull out the feathers, shake the loose tea out of his pockets and boots, and go to sleep.

Everybody did this except Paul Revere. Somebody had to ride to New York and Philadelphia to tell the colonists there what had just happened in Boston. Paul was the natural choice. By the time the report on the night's activities was prepared, Paul was in the saddle and ready to go. He barely had time to remove his disguise.

The trip to New York and Philadelphia and then back to Boston totaled three-hundred and fifty miles. It was the middle of the winter and travel conditions were not good. But Paul rode hard and furiously. He was back home in only eleven days!

ENGLAND
STRIKES BACK

—8—

When Paul Revere returned to Boston, he brought encouraging news with him. The leaders of the Sons of Liberty in Philadelphia and New York and the more radical of the Whigs there enthusiastically supported the "Boston Tea Party." They said they would not allow tea to be unloaded in their ports either. They also vowed to stand behind the people of Boston if that city was going to be punished after the news of the dumping reached London.

Although no one knew what the punishment would be, it was a certainty that Boston would have to "pay the piper" for the work of its "Mohawks." Some members of the Sons of Liberty actually hoped the British retaliation would be severe. They thought a harsh sentence might bring more colonists to their way of thinking.

It *was* a harsh sentence. And it came within a period of time not much longer than it took a ship to get from Boston to London and back.

Paul had returned to Boston at the end of December, 1773. Early in May of the following year, the British ship, the *Lively*, arrived full of soldiers and carrying the bad news that there was to be a blockade of the Boston harbor. No ships would be allowed in or out until the townspeople agreed to pay for the destroyed tea. In effect, Boston was going to have its food supply cut off.

In addition to closing the port, Parliament decided that Salem would replace Boston as the capital of the Massachusetts colony, and Plymouth would be the seat of customs. Parliament also declared that town meetings, which were a fixture of colonial life in New England, were forbidden.

To enforce these decisions, Parliament replaced the civilian governor, Hutchinson, with a military man, General Gage. Gage was known to the townspeople. He had been living there for a while and even had an American wife. He was considered to be a reasonable man and was well-liked too. But he had a job to do, and he set out with all determination to do it.

A few days after all Boston learned of the punishment, a mass meeting was held. The townspeople discussed the extent of the difficulties that lay ahead. They knew there would be serious problems. Since trade by sea was Boston's livelihood, clearly the seamen and merchants would be hit hard immediately. Then everybody else, in turn, would be

A British cartoon, published at the time the port of Boston was closed. The colonists were shown as slaves, convicted of capital crimes and caged.

hurt. The shopkeepers would be without goods, the artisans without customers, and the workers without jobs.

Paul Revere was again sent off to New York and Philadelphia with the news of Boston's plight. The Whigs in those two cities were sympathetic. They were united in support of Boston, as they feared that what happened in Boston could just as easily happen in their cities.

When Paul Revere returned home from his ride, he found the city infested with British soldiers. They were everywhere. One could not take a stroll without bumping into them. One could not pass a morning without hearing their drums. During the time of the Boston Massacre, there were only two regiments in town. Now there were eleven. Boston's streets were filled with thousands of scarlet uniforms.

General Gage had been doing his job. The cannon at Castle Island were ready to fire on any trading ships that entered or left the harbor. The port was now effectively shut down. The wharves, once alive with people and noise, were deserted. Gage had Boston in a stranglehold.

Fortunately for Boston residents, the colonies stuck together during these hard times. Money and supplies began arriving in Boston, by land, from up and down the coast. Wagons pulled into town carrying sacks of rice from South Carolina and bread from Maryland. Flour came in from Virginia. Sheep and sometimes droves of cattle were brought in from Connecticut. From the other Massachusetts towns came rye and wheat flour and salt codfish. Towns did what they could to help. Money even arrived from concerned citizens in England. (Not surprisingly, just as there were many colonists who favored British colonial rule, there were English people who supported the colonial Whigs' desire for political rights.) Boston's Tory faction was not without its English supporters. Money poured in from England to help them.

Meanwhile, Whig leaders worked to make sure the colonies kept in contact. Committees of Correspondence were formed for the purpose of getting letters and messages safely back and forth. Paul Revere was among the riders chosen to carry news from town to town. These couriers were trusted to get information to the right people and to relay the messages correctly.

The events leading to the British takeover of the port of Boston, and the occupation itself, divided the citizens. Fearing that a rebellion was brewing, some frightened Whigs moved out of town. Seeking the protection of the British soldiers, a number of Tories moved in. Paul Revere stayed right where he was, continuing to live on the square and keep up his shop near Clark's Wharf.

Former friends now became uneasy neighbors. People ignored each other on the streets. They were tense and troubled. Some of Paul's former friends and customers deserted him, thinking that his views on rights and liberties were treasonous. But, as he always had, Paul remained true to his beliefs. He remained greatly involved with the work of the Sons of Liberty.

Under the noses of the British regulars, Paul and the other Patriots continued to meet and plan their activities. More than ever before, they kept their meetings secret. Because there were just too many soldiers around, there were no more lively demonstrations. No more warpaint was worn, no more dummies were hung from trees. All protests were orderly. Most were in the form of newspaper editorials calling for representative government and freedom from foreign rule.

While the Tories avoided the Whigs and the Whigs avoided arrest, Gage's soldiers continued to be a menacing presence. One could see them drilling on just about any day in their well-cut uniforms with shining buttons. They snapped to attention as the officers barked out commands. With their flashing bayonets aimed frontward, they marched straight forward or slanted to the left or to the right. It was an impressive display and it was frightening. Children watched silently, spellbound. The time for insulting lone sentries was long gone.

READY AT A
MINUTE'S NOTICE

— 9 —

While the British regulars fine-tuned their military maneuvers in town, colonial "irregulars" were also preparing themselves by drilling in the country. These men had no special uniforms and they did not belong to famous regiments with glorious military histories. But they were well-armed with muskets and a knowledge and love of their land. They had hardened themselves to whatever had to be done. The American militia was ready to fight.

Some of these men were being specially prepared to be ready for action at a moment's notice. They slept in their upstairs bedrooms with their guns, bullets, and powder horns within easy reach. In a minute, they would be out of bed, dressed, down the stairs, and out in the street ready to join the fight. They were popularly known as Minute Men.

With military buildup going on intently on both sides, the threat of war was increasing. Patriot leaders in the

Massachusetts colony realized the clear need for support from the other colonies.

In 1774, the First Continental Congress, with Sam Adams and John Adams in attendance, met at Carpenters' Hall in Philadelphia. Meanwhile, back in Massachusetts, a county meeting was held. At that gathering, Joseph Warren drew up the Suffolk Resolves. This bold document stated that if British soldiers attacked the Massachusetts colony, the other twelve colonies would come to the aid of the militia.

The important document was handed to a trustworthy rider. Paul Revere was dispatched to Philadelphia with the papers. He rode swiftly to Carpenters' Hall and handed over the message he brought in his saddlebag.

The First Continental Congress passed the Suffolk Resolves.

Meanwhile, the militia was busy collecting and storing guns and kegs of gunpowder. Although they let their presence be known to the British troops, they tried to keep the location of their ammunition a secret.

The British army had a network of spies who were always trying to find out where the supplies were kept. When it was discovered that there was ammunition stored in Charlestown, a raiding party was sent to seize it. They did, and they returned to Boston before the militia could react.

To keep track of what the British and the British spies were up to, the Patriots developed their own network of spies. Paul Revere was one of them. The spies met in taverns. It was the job of these men to find out when the British were going to attempt another seizure.

Once, when Paul found out that the British were going to reinforce one of their forts in Portsmouth, New Hampshire, he quickly got word to the Minute Men in nearby Durham. They were able to ruin the mission by getting to that fort and taking it over before the British regulars left Boston. Shots were fired, but no one was hurt. But Paul caught the eye of the British. He was now under more careful observation.

Another time, he was much less successful. He was caught, along with others, while rowing in the vicinity of the Castle Island fort. Paul was forced to spend a few nights locked up in the fort. While he was there, he found out that another British expedition to raid Patriot supplies at Salem was afoot. He was frustrated that he could not be of help. Fortunately, the expedition turned out to be a failure, and those supplies hidden at Salem remained safe. Paul and the others were allowed to go back to Boston when the British soldiers returned.

Boston was a city full of Patriot and British spies. There were successes and failures on both sides. Artisans posed as country folk. British soldiers were disguised as farmers. Secret messages disappeared and meetings went unrecorded. Paul and his "committee" of spies roamed the streets at night. It was the winter of 1774–1775. It was the eve of war. Paul Revere was now forty years old.

THE MIDNIGHT RIDE

—10—

On March 5, 1775, a mass meeting was held at Old South Church. It was the latest in a series of yearly meetings to commemorate the Boston Massacre. This particular meeting was distinguished by the strong anti-British tone of the speeches. The key speaker was Joseph Warren. Sam Adams and John Hancock were also there.

It was courageous of those three colonial leaders to appear at such a meeting. Any one of them could have been arrested for treason and hung. That is what King George wanted. But General Gage was being careful. He had been putting off arresting Patriot leaders for fear of heating up the rebellion he had been trying to cool down. His only action on this day was to send a few young officers to the meeting to hear what was being said.

But soon the cautious general began to change his tactics. He decided that the time had come to put a firm stop to the Patriot activities and to take the leaders into custody. Aware of this, Sam Adams, John Hancock, and other important rebels left Boston for the safety of the countryside. Adams and Hancock went to Lexington. Dr. Joseph Warren remained in Boston, at great risk, continuing to see his patients by day and direct rebel activity in the evenings.

Through its spy network, the British army discovered that there was a large collection of military supplies, including cannon, stored in the farm village of Concord. They found out that ammunition was kept at Worcester as well. General Gage decided to seize the weapons at Concord. The failure of the earlier daytime expedition to take the supplies at Salem convinced him that this time the job must be done carefully and at night.

By Saturday, April 15, Paul Revere and the other rebel spies knew something was going on. They knew that hundreds of regulars were getting ready for transport. Transport boats had been seen on the Charles River, and British scouts had been spotted on the roads to Lexington and Concord. On Sunday, Paul rode up to Lexington to warn Adams and Hancock. Also, the Minute Men at Concord were advised of the expected British troop movement. The Patriots knew they had to hide the ammunition and be prepared for action.

Gage was trying to be thorough in his plans to stop the colonial express riders from passing along the times and directions of troop movements. Officers were positioned along the land routes to Lexington and Concord. The British man-of-war, the *Somerset*, took its place in the Charles River to prevent rebel spies from crossing there and taking the Charlestown route to Lexington. Gage wanted the move on Concord to be a surprise.

Paul Revere and the network of Patriot spies knew, of course, all about the British plans. They held some meetings at Joseph Warren's house to make plans of their own. They decided at those meetings that two riders would try to get out of Boston and up to Lexington and Concord to signal the Minute Men. William Dawes, who, unlike Revere, was not a marked man, would leave through the town gate. Paul would try to sneak across the Charles River in a rowboat, then go the rest of the way on horseback.

Paul suggested a set of signals to be given to the men waiting for him with a saddled horse on the other side of the river in Charlestown. He decided that if the British were going to go toward Concord by boat, two lanterns should be hung from the spire of Boston North Church. If the British troop movement was on land, one lantern would be hung. The men would be able to see the lanterns from across the river. If the two riders did not get through, at least *some* warning would have been given. Robert Newman, the twenty-three-year-old sexton of Boston North Church, was going to hang the lanterns. He lived across the street from the church and had a set of keys.

Paul went home and told his family what he was going to do. They knew that he was about to risk his life and all he had for the cause he believed in. There was no doubt that what he was set to do was an act of treason. But the Patriots needed him and he would not let them down.

On Tuesday, April 18, North Square was filled with regulars equipped for battle. As darkness set in that night, they were lining up at the dock to ship out. At 10:00 P.M., Joseph Warren gave the signal for Dawes and Revere to go.

Paul left his house in a hurry. His dog, which followed him out the door, scampered along behind him. The sexton

*During his famous ride, Revere warning
the colonists that the British were coming*

of North Church, Robert Newman, was upstairs in his house pretending to be asleep. Downstairs, a group of British officers who were quartered there were busy playing cards and drinking. Paul signaled to him, and Newman climbed out a window. Paul instructed the young sexton to hang two lanterns. He told him to hang them well apart so they could be clearly seen. Newman climbed the steps to the highest window in the church tower. He climbed way up, past the eight great bells that Paul used to ring as a boy. He then lit the lanterns as he was told.

Once this was done, Paul, still followed by his dog, hustled down to the river where two friends were waiting to row him across. They used a rowboat that had been hidden near the Charlestown ferry port.

In his haste, Paul made two mistakes: he left his spurs at home, and he forgot to bring cloth to muffle the sounds of the oars. To get the spurs, Paul did a clever thing. He wrote a note to Rachel and tied it to his faithful dog's collar. He then sent the dog home and waited. Soon it returned, wagging its tail. The spurs were wrapped around its collar!

To get the cloth, one of Paul's two friends went to the home of his girlfriend, which happened to be nearby. He called up to her and told her what he needed. She promptly stepped out of her flannel petticoat and tossed it out the window.

Now that the three men had everything they needed, it was time to go. They rowed silently on that moonlit night, keeping as far away from the sixty-four guns of the *Somerset* as they could. Fortunately, they were neither seen nor heard. The little boat made it safely across.

Signal lanterns in the belfry of North Church

Across the river, the men waiting in the shadows in Charlestown had indeed seen Newman's signal. Paul was given the best Yankee horse Charlestown had. He mounted the fine, quick, slender animal and began the ride of his life. It was only about twelve miles to Lexington and about five more to Concord. But Paul was riding further than that. This stocky, middle-aged silversmith was about to ride into the history and folklore of a new nation.

At the point where Paul began his ride, the Charles River was on his left and the Mystic River was on his right. There were two roads, and Paul took the one that went to Lexington by way of Cambridge. Having just been there on the previous Sunday, he knew the route well.

Paul was concerned with being ambushed, so he kept at a steady but rapid trot, always shifting his eyes from left to right. He kept a sharp eye out so he could spot the British patrols before they spotted him. Although his most important task was to get to Lexington and warn Adams and Hancock, he would also try to awaken a few families along the way so the alarm could begin spreading. We do not know exactly what Paul was thinking about as he rode, but he must have known that all his earlier rides were of small importance compared to this one.

Before long, Paul's sharp eyes picked out two British officers on horseback up ahead. He immediately galloped off across the countryside, making his way toward the other road he knew led to Lexington. On his light, fast horse, he quickly outdistanced his pursuers. He was safe, for now.

When he reached Lexington, he was welcomed into the house where Hancock and Adams were staying. He told the two leaders that more than one thousand regulars were heading that way by boat. He told them that the countryside was being alerted. Perhaps the signals of guns firing and bells ringing could even be heard. About half an hour later, William Dawes arrived. The group sat down to eat. Then Paul Revere, Dawes, and a young doctor named Samuel Prescott rode off to Concord to warn the Minute Men there, and to warn more farmers along the way.

They got about halfway to Concord when Paul was stopped by a group of six British officers. Soon he was surrounded by still more officers. Dawes and Prescott, who were a few hundred yards away, escaped. Dawes lost his horse and hid in the bushes, but Dr. Prescott managed to ride ahead to Concord.

Paul was questioned at gunpoint. He told the officers who he was and what he had done. He boldly explained to them that an alarm had been sounded and that armed Minute Men were fully aroused and flooding the countryside.

The British officers knew whom they had captured. They told Paul they would blow his brains out if he tried to escape. Facing the pistol squarely, Paul replied that they could do as they pleased. He knew he had done his job.

Paul was forced to turn over his horse. But he was held prisoner for only a short while. When the officers fully realized the trouble they were in, they let him go. They figured it would be much easier to make their escape without having to drag a prisoner along. The soldiers took Paul's horse with them and disappeared down the road.

THE WAR
FOR INDEPENDENCE

— 11 —

Exhausted, but exhilarated, Paul wondered for a minute what to do next. He decided not to go on to Concord. Instead, he chose to walk back across the countryside to Lexington, to see if Hancock and Adams were still there and to see what he could do to help them. When he finally reached Lexington, it was nearly dawn.

The two Patriot leaders were still there, but were preparing to leave town when Paul arrived. And there *was* something else Paul could do, something very important. Hancock had left a large trunk in a second floor room of Buckman's Tavern. Inside the trunk were important papers. The trunk had to be taken and hidden from the British soldiers. Paul and Hancock's clerk, John Lowell, volunteered to retrieve the trunk.

When Paul got to the tavern, which was located on Lexington green, he went right upstairs. Looking out at the green from an upstairs window, he saw a handful of Minute

Men forming into a group of some kind in the gray, early morning mist. The group became a raggedy battleline. There were fifty or sixty of these men standing there. Some had muskets. Some were unarmed. Paul and John Lowell got the trunk out.

As the two left the tavern carrying the heavy trunk, the orderly regiments of the British army were systematically filing onto the green in their splendid white and scarlet uniforms and full battle gear. The soldiers and their mounted officers stood in perfect order opposite the plainly dressed and poorly armed farmers. There was some talk between the opposing commanders. Then a shot was fired, followed by a loud shout, followed by a volley of shots.

That was all Paul saw and heard. He was busy getting the trunk to a safe place.

The skirmish was over almost as soon as it began. Eight Minute Men were killed and ten others were wounded. Two British regulars received slight bullet wounds. To this day, it is not known who fired first.

The British soldiers were jubilant as they marched on to Concord. Cooped up in Boston for so long, they were eager for action. They were soon to get all the action they could stand. At North Bridge in Concord, the regulars were met not by a handful of men, but by hundreds of them.

The Minute Men shot at the British troops as they made a hasty retreat back to Boston. The angry and proud farmers shot from behind barns and stone walls. They fired from the bushes and from behind trees. The slaughter of the redcoats increased as more and more militiamen joined the fight along the way.

The regulars, in full retreat and exhausted, eventually

The Battle of Lexington

made it back to Boston. It was past midnight. One out of every nine British soldiers had been killed. The British reinforcements that arrived did their share of damage as well. The war for American independence had begun.

The revolution spread rapidly to all the other thirteen colonies. But it took the American colonists six and a half years of fighting to gain their independence from England. It took the help of the French. It took the fact that England was involved in military action all over the world. But mostly it took the courage, determination, and perserverence of the people in those thirteen colonies.

Paul Revere told the colonial leaders that he was ready to serve in any capacity, that he would do whatever was needed.

Artillery was needed. Paul learned to make cannon from a French cannon maker.

Gunpowder was needed. Paul rode to Philadelphia where he quickly learned how to make it. Then he returned north and supervised the setting up of a powder mill.

Money was needed. Paul engraved copper plates for the printing of paper money. He designed the official colonial seal, too.

The colonies needed express riders as well. For five shillings a day, Paul rode for the Boston Committee of Safety.

But the colonies did not need silver bowls and teapots, nor did they need picture frames or pet collars. Paul did little silversmithing during the war.

He did, however, put his knowledge of dentistry to good use one time. It happened months after the Battle of Bunker Hill, at which the great Patriot leader, Dr. Joseph Warren, was killed. A body, thought to be Warren's, was unearthed. Paul was able to identify it by studying the teeth. He recognized the two false teeth he had placed and the silver wire with which he had fastened them. This was important, because now Warren could get the distinguished funeral he so deserved. The young doctor who gave his life for the revolution was only thirty-four when he died. Paul grieved for his dear lifelong friend.

Paul did whatever was asked of him during the war years. He achieved good results with almost everything he did. But he never had quite the same successes in his military career.

For a while, he was given command of the fort at Castle Island, once the British left Boston. There was not much for him to do there. Nonetheless, he was given a high rank in the Massachusetts militia.

Paul did take part in a few military expeditions without distinguishing himself. In fact, for his efforts during one campaign at Penobscot, Maine, he was accused of cowardice. He was later thoroughly cleared of the charge.

MORE
THAN A LEGEND

—12—

The fighting ended in 1783 when a treaty was signed. Paul was forty-eight years old and ready to get back to his silversmith work. But he had many mouths to feed. He opened a hardware store, too.

The store was a great success. He sold goods he made and others he imported. He sold everything from toupees to sleigh bells. He sold many decks of playing cards. He also sold the finest cloth available. Boston residents were in need of eyeglasses. He sold them, too.

Perhaps Paul's store was successful because of its patriotic location—right across from where the Liberty Tree once stood! It is much more likely, however, that Paul's prosperity was due to his skills as a businessman and to the rapid growth of the city of Boston, with its new and greater demands. He soon moved the store to a new location near Faneuil Hall.

Throughout his life, Paul was always able to adapt to

Faneuil Hall in Boston in the 1780s

changes and learn to do what was needed. The young country needed a navy at that time, and ships to go with it. Ship bottoms needed copper sheathing. Paul, who knew a lot about copper, learned to roll sheet copper to be used on the ships. In 1800, Paul purchased property in Canton, Massachusetts, and set up a copper mill. He called the property Canton Dale. The land also had a house on it.

He soon developed quite a talent for rolling copper. He made the copper sheathing for the famous American warship the *Constitution*. It was Paul Revere who gave the dome of the Boston statehouse a copper covering. He did the same for the New York city hall and other public buildings. It was Paul who worked on the copper boiler on Robert Fulton's steamship. In fact, it can be argued that Paul's work in copper was his greatest contribution to his country.

Another thing Paul did very well was make bells. He made about four hundred of them. One of the biggest and most famous of his bells is still hanging in the tower of King's Chapel in Boston. Today, others can be seen and heard in church steeples throughout New England. In 1804, Paul moved his bell foundry to Canton Dale.

Paul made a great deal of money as he got older. He moved his family to a large house on Charter Street. But excelling at something was important to Paul, more important than making money. During his lifetime, he was considered just about the best silversmith, copper manufacturer, and bell maker In America!

Toward the end of his long, healthy life, Paul Revere spent more and more time living in the house in Canton Dale. He loved the country. He loved its sounds and its smells. He loved to take walks. He began to write poetry to express his happiness. In these poems, he wrote about how much he enjoyed the company of his friends and neighbors.

One of his friends was a woman named Deborah Gannett. When Paul knew her, she was middle-aged, married, and the mother of three children. When she was much younger, and her name was Deborah Sampson, she had disguised herself as a boy and fought bravely for the Continental Army in the Revolutionary War. Now, she and her family were poor, and she was in bad health. On her behalf, Paul wrote a letter to Congress that resulted in her receiving a military pension.

Another thing Paul loved to do was to spend his evenings with his many grandchildren and great-grandchildren, telling them stories of the days when he rode express for the Sons of Liberty. One story he told was about the night of his ride to Lexington, when his dog brought the spurs, and a woman's petticoat muffled the oars of the rowboat.

In 1813, Paul had his portrait painted again. This time the artist was Gilbert Stuart. The painting showed Paul with a double chin and white hair. But it also showed that same bold, self-satisfied look Copley captured almost half a century earlier. Rachel Revere had her portrait painted as well.

A few months later, Rachel died at the age of sixty-eight. Paul was greatly saddened.

This must have been a time of reflection for Paul Revere. He was one of the last of the Patriot leaders still alive. Sam Adams, John Hancock, Joseph Warren, and Josiah Quincy were gone. So was William Dawes. And Boston had changed so much. Trees were being cut down, hills leveled, and bays and coves filled as the city expanded. Street names were changed, especially to erase any suggestion of British domination, and some of the buildings Revere knew were gone.

But the memories remained. Paul kept on being a patriot to his last days. He even wore the clothing of those colonial times. And he never told anyone that he was with the mob dumping tea that night on Griffin's Wharf. After all, he had sworn an oath of secrecy.

On Sunday, May 10, 1818, Paul Revere died at the age of eighty-three. It seems fitting that he died on a Sunday, a day on which the bells he loved—and some that he made—would be ringing all over Boston.

APPENDIX
IMPORTANT DATES
DURING THE
AMERICAN REVOLUTION

Summer of 1774   First Continental Congress convenes. Laws and ordinances passed. Committees established.

April 19, 1775   Battle of Lexington and Concord, the first battle fought in the American Revolution (eight Americans killed, ten wounded).

May 1775   Second Continental Congress convenes. Congress takes stronger stand against British in order to defend rights.

May 10, 1775   Capture of Ticonderoga. American capture of Fort

Ticonderoga, New York, without a shot fired, gives the Americans control of Lake Champlain and opens Canada to invasion from the south.

June 17, 1775

Battle of Bunker Hill fought on the Charleston Peninsula, across from the Charles River around Boston. Major action occurs at Breed's Hill, southeast of Bunker Hill. Heavy British casualties.

July 8, 1775

"Olive Branch Petition" sent to King George III is not accepted by him. This petition represents the last chance at peace.

December 1775

Prohibitory Act passed by British Parliament creates naval blockade of America, seizure of American goods on the seas. This further unites Americans to the cause of independence.

December 30, 1775

Battle of Quebec. Fought in Canada, this battle results in over half of the American force being killed, wounded, or captured. British hold strong position in Canada.

January 1776	Thomas Paine's *Common Sense* is published. It calls forth the intense need to separate from England.
March 17, 1776	The British abandon Boston to the Americans permanently.
July 4, 1776	The Declaration of Independence is officially sanctioned by Congress. The thirteen colonies become the United States of America.
August 27–28, 1776	Battle fought in Brooklyn, New York. British successfully invade New York City, causing Washington to abandon that area.
December 25–26, 1776	General George Washington crosses the Delaware River and attacks Hessian garrison at Trenton.
January 3, 1777	Washington successfully attacks Princeton, giving Americans a small but important victory.
October 4, 1777	Battle of Germantown. British occupy Philadelphia, but the city is found not to be of strategic importance, and Washington's army remains intact.

October 7, 1777	American troops defeat British at Saratoga, New York. France enters the war as an ally of America.
Winter 1777–1778	Washington's army suffers losses from cold, exposure, disease, and hunger at Valley Forge, near Philadelphia.
June 28, 1778	Battle of Monmouth. Fought in New Jersey, 50 miles (80 km) northeast of Philadelphia. Neither side clearly wins, although the British are able to move into New York safely.
February 23–24, 1779	George Rogers Clark leads expedition against the British, capturing the towns of Kaskaskia, Illinois, and Vincennes, Indiana. These and other British defeats establish American control of the old Northwest— the lands between the Great Lakes and the Ohio River.
October 9, 1799	Battle of Savannah. British victory allows them to attack South Carolina.
April 1–May 12, 1780	British siege of Charleston, South Carolina. Heavy Amer-

ican losses. British occupy
South Carolina.

October 7, 1780 — Battle of King's Mountain,
fought in South Carolina, about
thirty miles (48 km) west of
Charlotte, North Carolina. This
American victory causes the
British to retreat to Camden,
South Carolina.

January 17, 1781 — Battle at Cowpens, in South
Carolina. British suffer losses
and are kept from overrunning
North Carolina.

March 1, 1781 — Articles of Confederation
officially ratified.

September 28–
October 19, 1781 — Battle of Yorktown. The final
and decisive battle of the
American Revolution, in which
the British forces surrender to
Washington.

September 3, 1783 — Peace of Paris—the British-
American peace treaty—
becomes final.

May 25–
September 17, 1787 — Constitutional Convention
meets in Philadelphia.

June 21, 1788 — Constitution is adopted.

FOR
FURTHER READING

Collier, James Lincoln, and Christopher Collier. *My Brother Sam is Dead*. New York: Four Winds Press, 1974.

Dickinson, Alice. *The Stamp Act*. New York: Franklin Watts, Inc., 1970.

Forbes, Esther. *Johnny Tremain*. Boston: Houghton Mifflin, 1943.

Fritz, Jean. *Early Thunder*. New York: Coward-McCann, Inc., 1967.

McGovern, Ann. *The Secret Soldier—The Story of Deborah Sampson*. New York: Scholastic, Inc., 1977.

Millender, Dharathula H. *Crispus Attucks: Black Leader of Colonial Patriots*. Bobbs-Merrill, 1965.

Sloane, Eric. *A Museum of Early American Tools*. New York: Ballantine Books, 1985.

INDEX

ABOUT
THE AUTHOR

Martin Lee is a writer and educator living with his wife, Marcia Miller, in New York City. He is also a partner in a company that develops educational materials.